The Bare Naked

Book

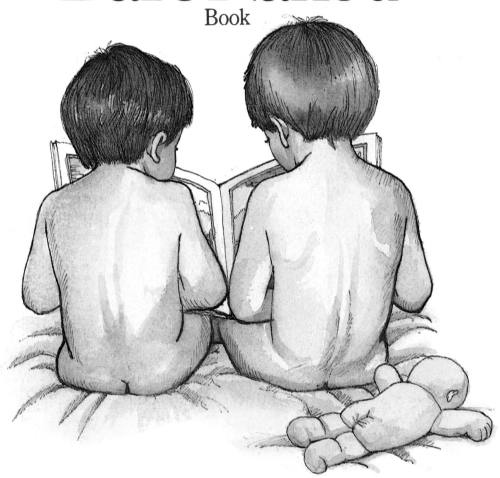

Written by Kathy Stinson

Illustrated by Heather Collins

Annick Press Ltd.
Toronto • New York • Vancouver

Tenth printing, September 1999

Annick Press Ltd.

We acknowledge the support of the Canada
Council for the Arts for our publishing program.
We also thank the Ontario Arts Council.

Cataloguing in Publication Data
    Stinson, Kathy
        The bare naked book

    (Annick toddler series)
    ISBN 0-920303-52-8 (bound) ISBN 0-920303-53-6 (pbk.)

    I. Collins, Heather. II. Title. III. Series.

    PS8587.T56B37 1986 jC813'.54 C85-090837-X
    PZ7.S74Ba 1986

Distributed in Canada by:
Firefly Books Ltd.
3680 Victoria Park Avenue
Willowdale, ON
M2H 3K1

Published in the U.S.A. by Annick Press (U.S.) Ltc
Distributed in the U.S.A. by:
Firefly Books (U.S.) Inc.
P.O. Box 1338
Ellicott Station
Buffalo, NY 14205

Printed and bound in Canada by
Friesens, Altona, Manitoba.

A special story for Jessica and Shane Fenton
and for Peter and Baby Koven

Bodies

Running bodies ... Swimming bodies

Jumping bodies ... Stretching bodies ...

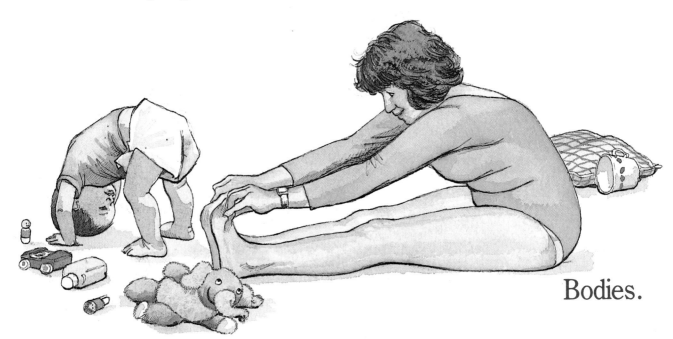

Bodies.

Hair

Dripping
hair

Straight hair

Curly hair

Tangled
hair

Hair...

Where
is
your
hair?

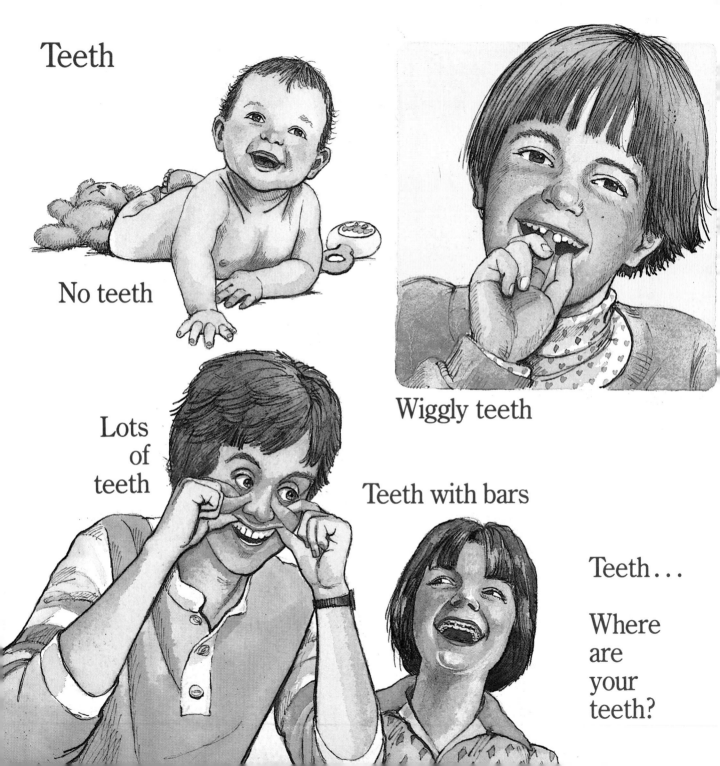

Teeth

No teeth

Wiggly teeth

Lots
of
teeth

Teeth with bars

Teeth...

Where
are
your
teeth?

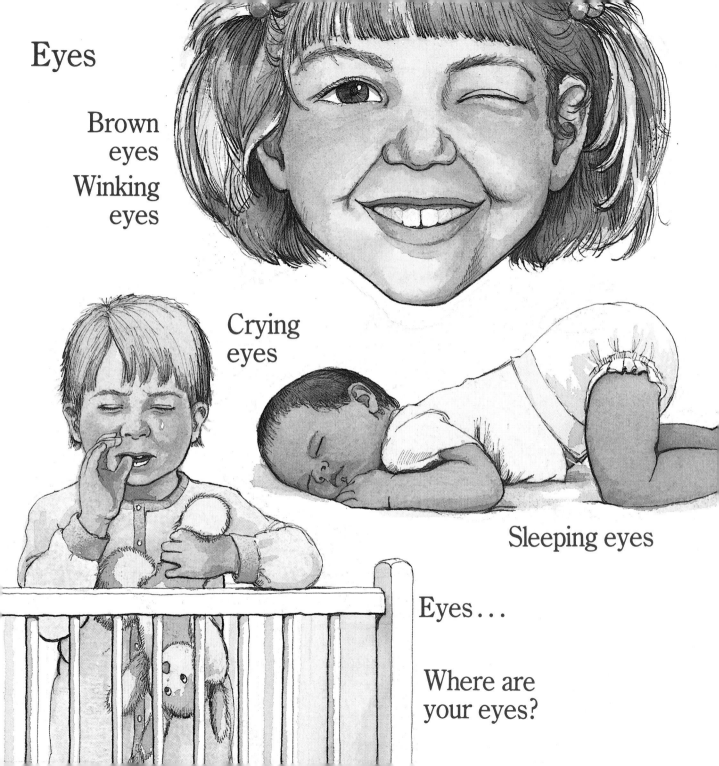

Eyes

Brown
eyes
Winking
eyes

Crying
eyes

Sleeping eyes

Eyes . . .

Where are
your eyes?

Green and
purple tongues

Tastes-
yucky
tongues

Tongues . . . Where is your tongue?

Tongues

Licking
tongues

Slurping
tongues

Noses

Runny noses

Itchy noses

Blowing noses

Don't pick your nose

Noses . . .

Where is your nose?

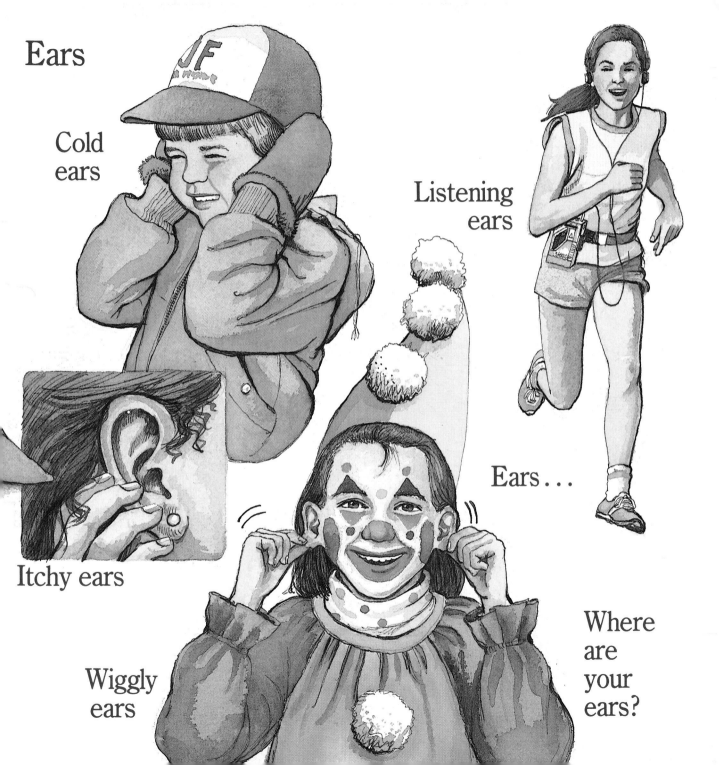

Ears

Cold
ears

Listening
ears

Itchy ears

Ears . . .

Wiggly
ears

Where
are
your
ears?

Shoulders

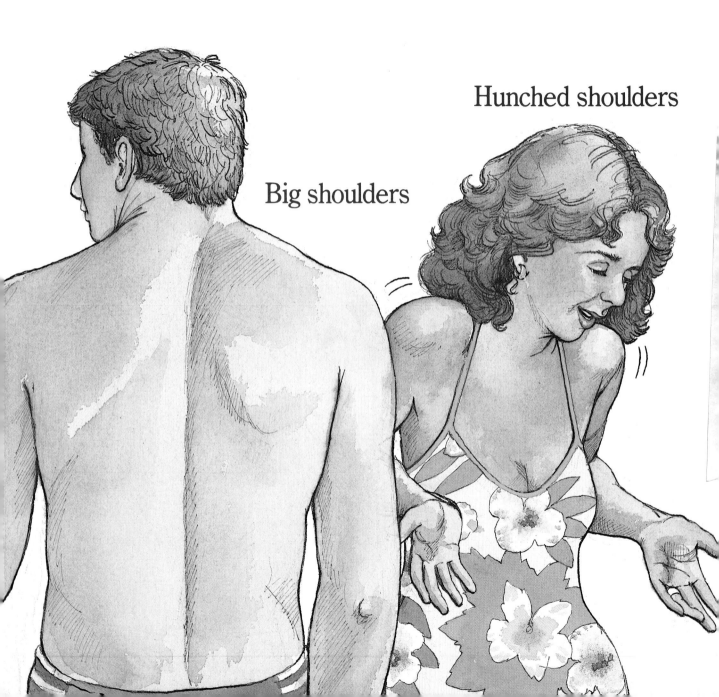

Big shoulders

Hunched shoulders

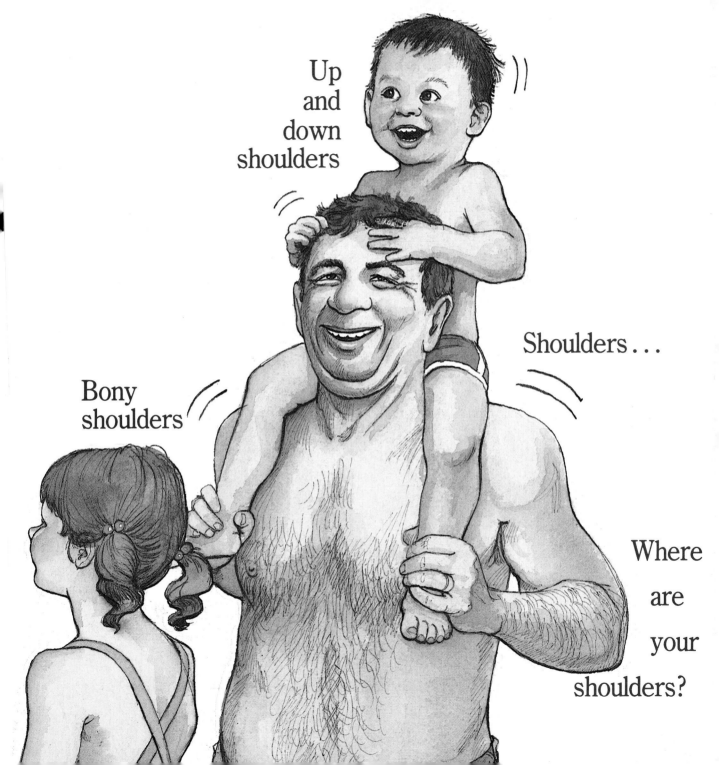

Belly buttons

In-a-lump belly buttons

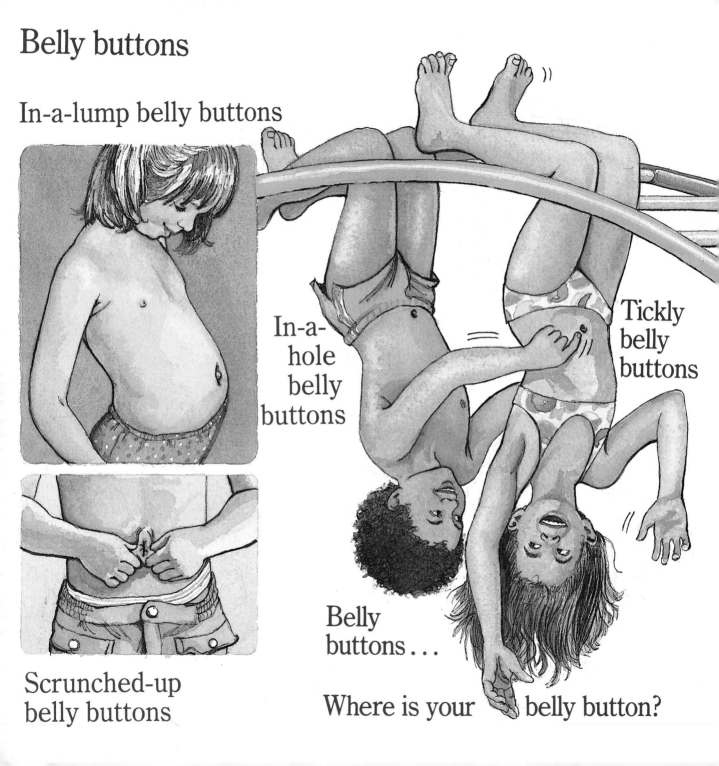

In-a-hole belly buttons

Tickly belly buttons

Scrunched-up belly buttons

Belly buttons . . .

Where is your belly button?

Nipples

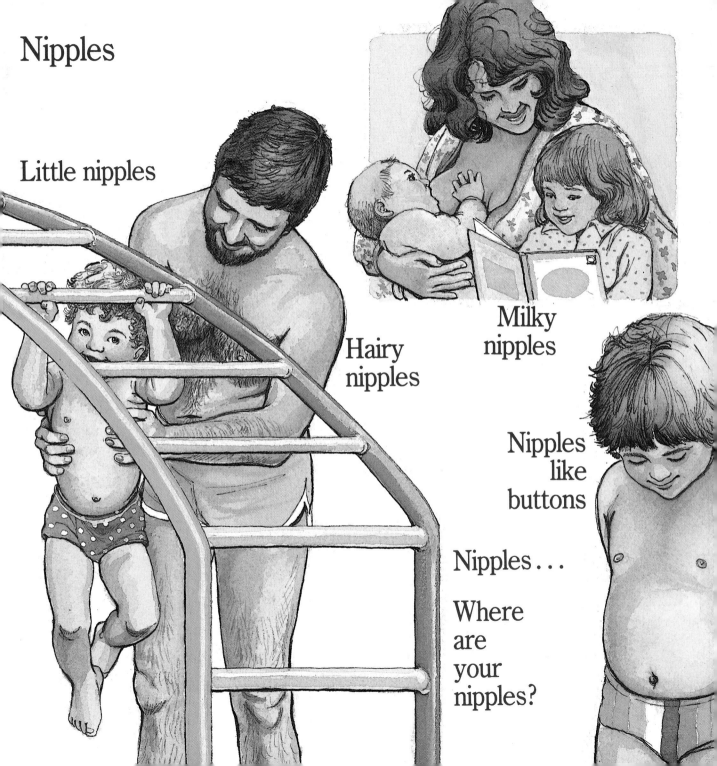

Little nipples

Hairy
nipples

Milky
nipples

Nipples
like
buttons

Nipples . . .

Where
are
your
nipples?

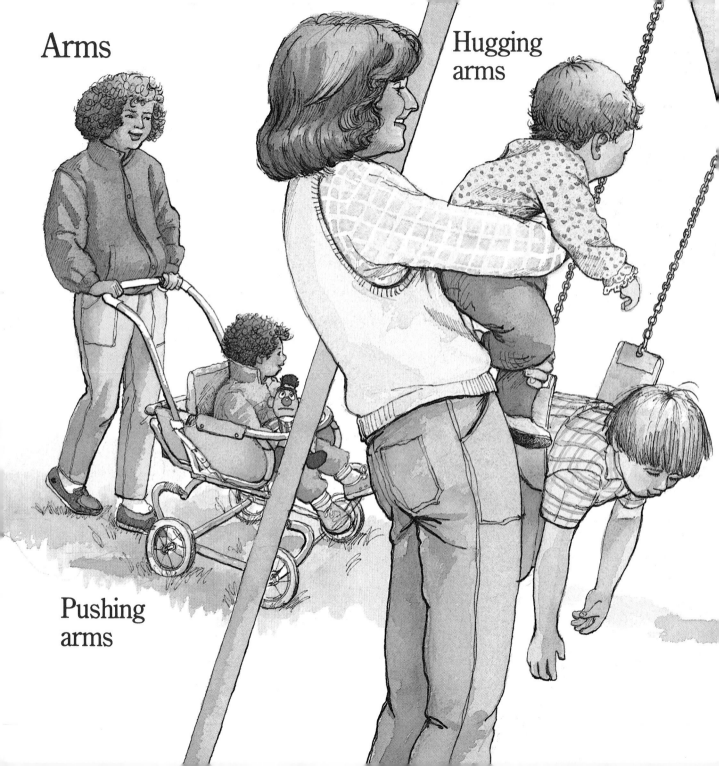

Arms

Hugging arms

Pushing arms

Lifting arms

Swinging arms

Arms...

Where are your arms?

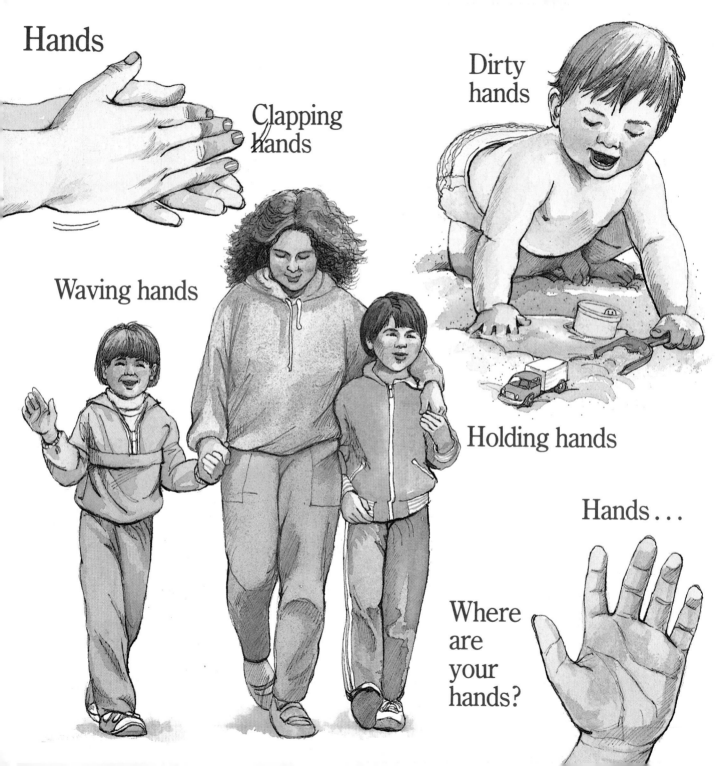

Hands

Clapping hands

Dirty hands

Waving hands

Holding hands

Hands . . .

Where are your hands?

Fingers

Poking fingers

Pinched fingers

Wiggling fingers

Sucking fingers

Fingers...

Where are your fingers?

Penises   That's
           for
           boys

Penises...

Where
is
your
penis?

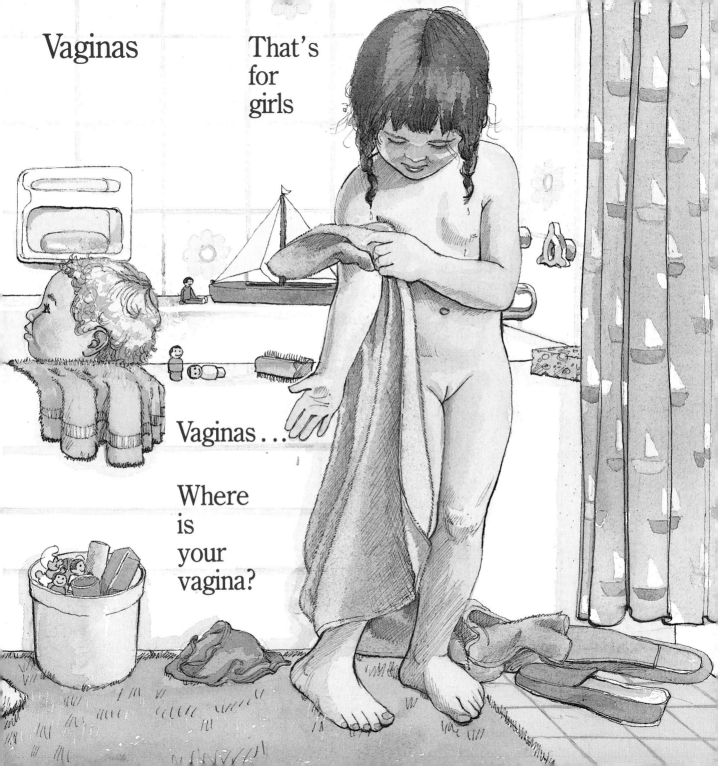

Vaginas

That's for girls

Vaginas . . .

Where is your vagina?

Bums

Standing-up bums

Sitting-down bums

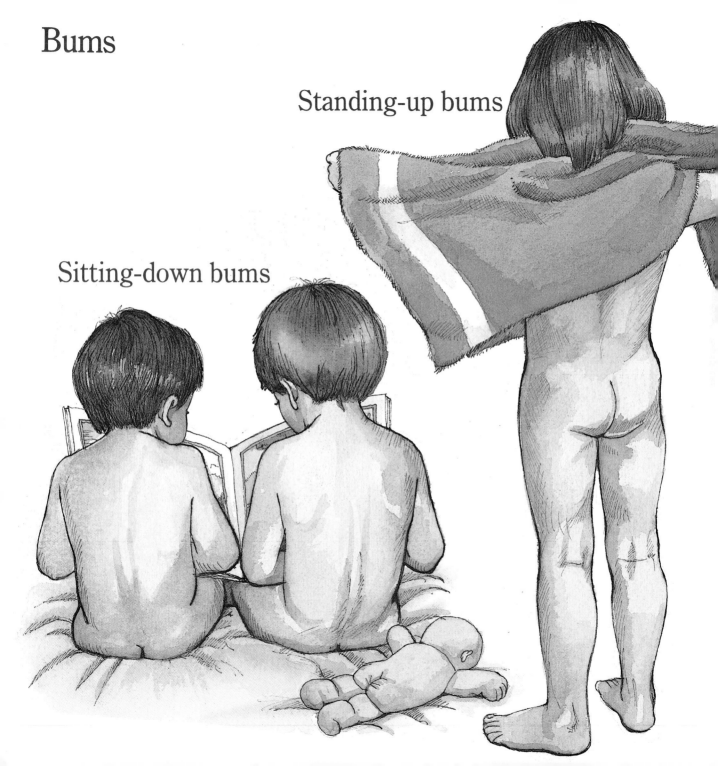

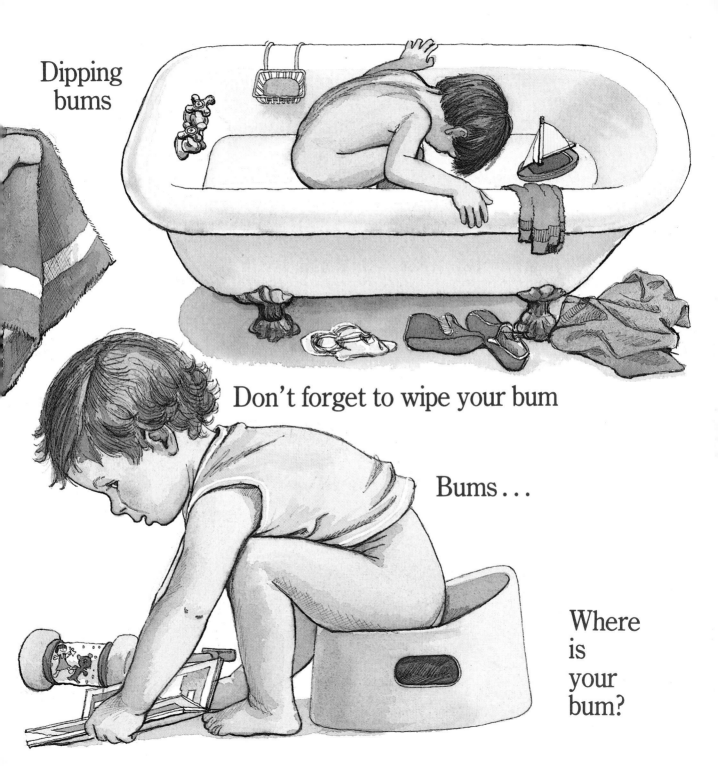

Dipping
bums

Don't forget to wipe your bum

Bums...

Where
is
your
bum?

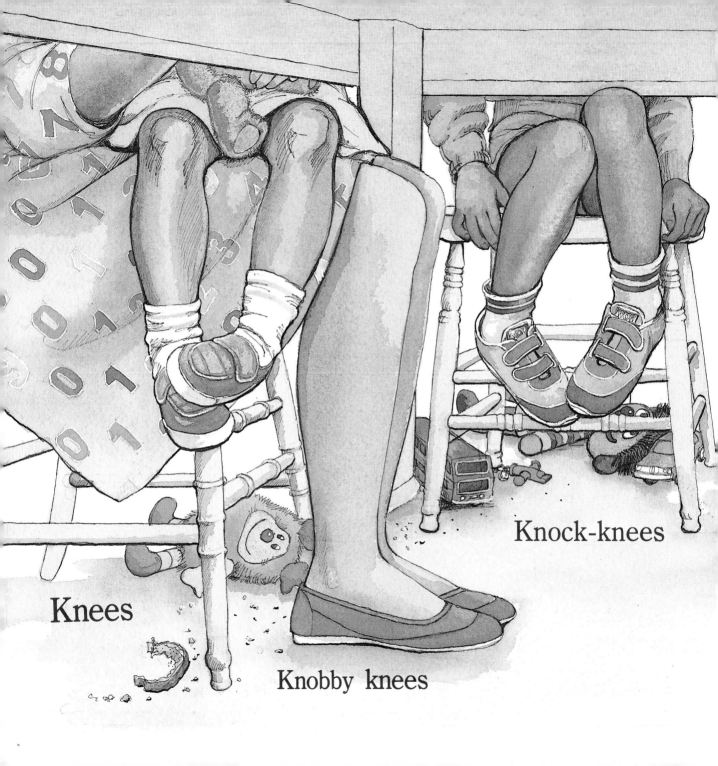

Knees

Knobby knees

Knock-knees

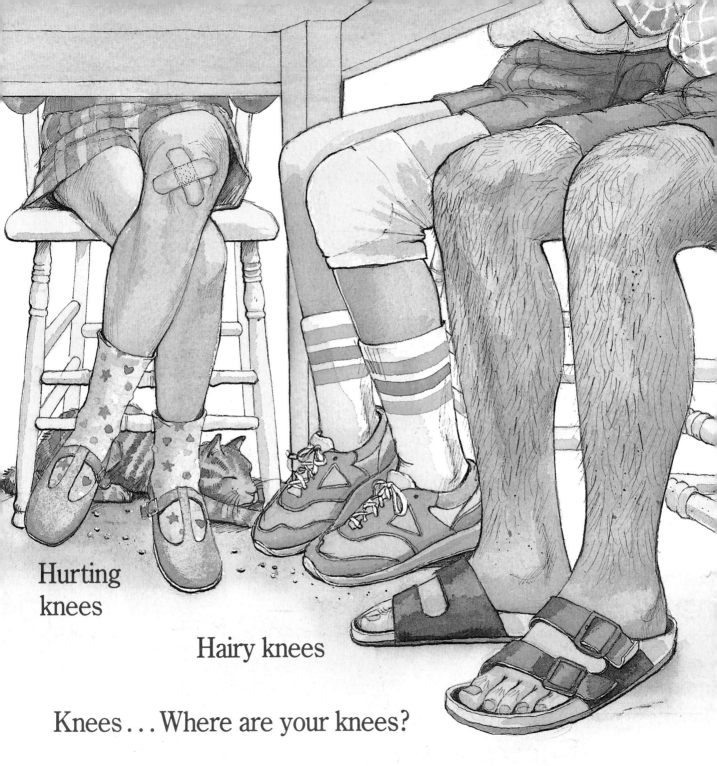

Hurting
knees

Hairy knees

Knees . . . Where are your knees?

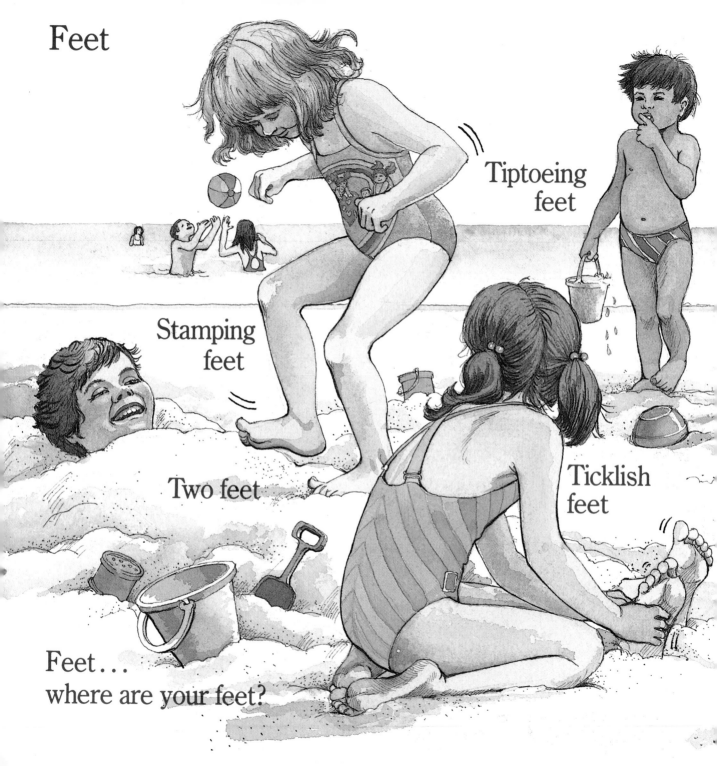

Feet

Tiptoeing feet

Stamping feet

Two feet

Ticklish feet

Feet...
where are your feet?

Toes

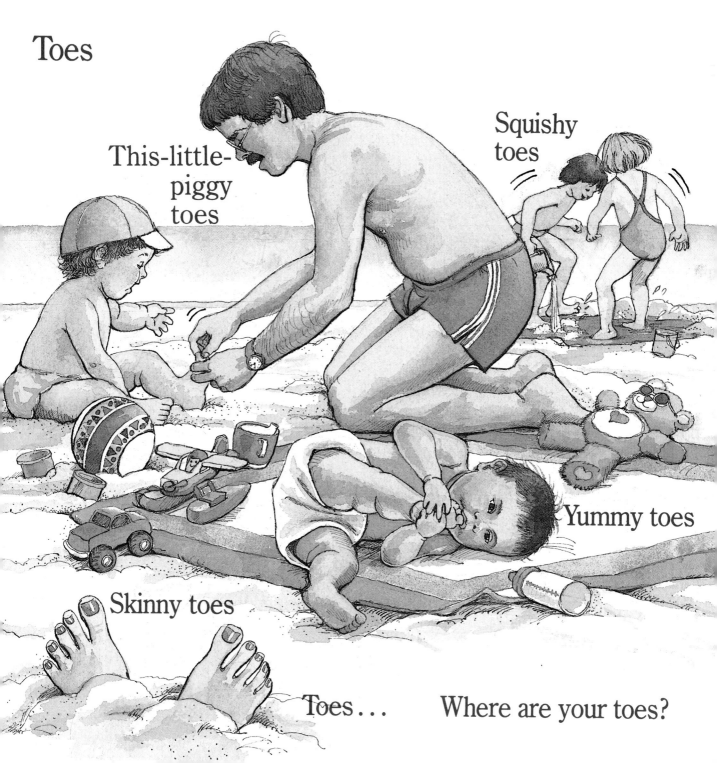

This-little-piggy toes

Squishy toes

Yummy toes

Skinny toes

Toes ...

Where are your toes?

Bodies

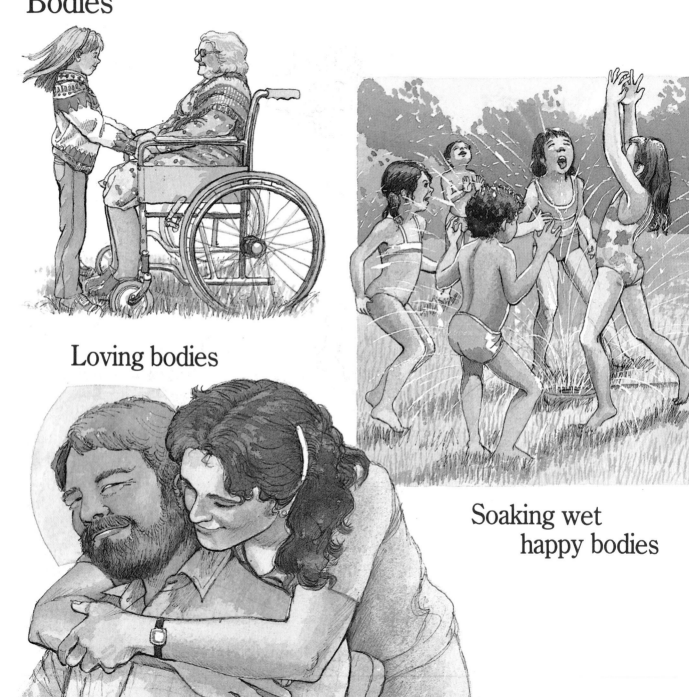

Loving bodies

Soaking wet
happy bodies

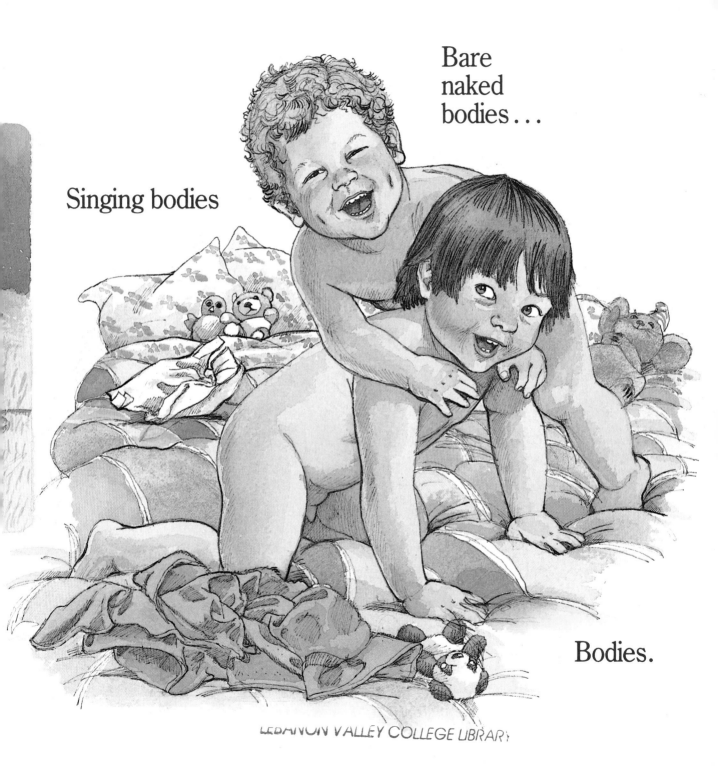

Singing bodies

Bare
naked
bodies . . .

Bodies.